PJ RAE

Strength Training After Age 50

Build (or Rebuild) Your Strongest Body: For Men and Women

Contents

1

INTRODUCTION

This book is intended for a particular generation: those of us past the golden age of 50. If that's you, then you've found the right tome to get you into the shape you want for the rest of the journey. That's what this is: a journey, and that's how we'll be referring to it throughout the rest of this book. Hopefully, this will be a journey that doesn't end; that makes it an adventure.

Who am I to be so bold as to pen this ditty? I'm someone who's been training in one form or another since I was 14 years old. I've done weights, Nautilus, bands, yoga, body weight, running, swimming, and probably some other stuff I can't think of right now. I was a personal trainer before they had a name for it, and I've lost count of how many people I've worked with over the years. Oh, and by the way, I'm old enough to have grandchildren, so I've been around the block a time or two. This topic is in my wheelhouse, so hold on tight.

You likely already have a good base of knowledge regarding exercise; you're familiar with the gym and the various workouts for different body parts. If not, no worries. We'll get into those movements in further chapters and show a few illustrations of some that you may not be familiar with. For purposes of this book, we focus primarily on weights: plates, bars, and dumbbells. Yes, there are lots of other protocols, but if you want to build strength, this is your first stop. Trust us, it works. The yoga and cardio books are somewhere else, not here. This is where you'll crush cans and stuff.

This will be a little different from the usual guides available for workouts, and let's be honest, there are plenty of them available. Our big difference is that we're going to be introspective, and hopefully a little entertaining as well.

Before we get into the actual workouts, we're going to discuss how to make those workouts successful. After all, if you've invested this much effort then let's ensure it pays off.

Most people that undertake strength training, as opposed to other types of conditioning programs do so because they realize how much strength and endurance they've lost over the years. Family and job responsibilities probably cost enough time that previous high levels of activity got prioritized out...and the weight gain came in as the strength adiosed. Now the kids are grown and maybe off to college and suddenly your life is your own again. Awesome. Let's get going.

Basically, getting the most out of your workouts means that you have a plan, and in this case, the plan starts in your head, and then to your body.

Of course, you can skip this part and just jump ahead to the program, but do yourself a favor and indulge in this. I promise it'll be worth your time. You can thank me later with an awesome review (seriously: we need awesome reviews).

Chapter 1 Setting Goals and Expectations

This part is very important. So important that you want to write this down, preferably in a journal that you'll keep handy and refer back to frequently. If you seriously want to get into strength training, you'll need this foundation to build upon. (This is yours; no need to share with anyone unless you want to.)

Following are the things you'll be writing in said journal:

1. What is it you want to accomplish with this program? In other words, what are your goals here?
2. When do you want to arrive at your goals? One month? Six months? A year? Be realistic.
3. What are you willing to do to accomplish your goals? Again: be realistic.
4. **Why** do you want to achieve these goals? This is the big one, and the one you'll really need to think about. In other words: what is your <u>reason</u>? Is it enough to keep you focused?

As a sort of guide to help you think about these things, I'll cite a few examples along the way, using an actual 'gym rat' I have known over the years.

Lou was a guy who was on the trading desk of the Stock Exchange...back when there was such a thing. Very successful but very busy and stressed out. Lou developed what we affectionately called a 'Dunlap', as in a spare tire around his middle. He'd also atrophied quite a bit because of a lack of any type of real exercise over the years. So, once he was able to retrieve some time, he decided to also retrieve his body and he put together his plan. In a nutshell, here's what that looked like.

Accomplish: lose the 'Dunlap', which he estimated to be about 20 pounds. Build up the atrophied muscles in his arms, legs, chest, and back. He listed some milestones along the way, e.g. bench press ¾ of his body weight by the ninth month, squat his body weight by the sixth month, etc. As he reached each milestone, he'd adjust them accordingly.

Time: Lou gave himself a year. After all, it took him 20+ to get himself 'lumpy', as he called it.

Commitment: Lou started with a four-day/week plan, and would increase to six days in or within 6 months. Each workout would last as close to 45 minutes as he could make it, depending on the day's plan. This is interesting, and we'll talk more about that in later chapters.

Why: Lou put together quite an essay on his 'why', starting with his marriage and commitment to being the best husband he could be. Certainly, he wanted to look better without his shirt on, feel better overall, and rebuild the energy he once had. What I found most compelling in his 'why' was his concern about his loved ones and how much that motivated him to get on his journey. Lou later admitted to me that going through the 'why' part of this exercise became an epiphany for him in terms of dealing with the 'back nine' of life. Good stuff.

I can't emphasize enough the importance of taking the time to go through this process. It's an exercise for sure, but a mental one and will pay dividends in your journey. Give this a serious effort, and you're going to be surprised at your own insights.

Just do it (do I owe Nike anything?).

3

Chapter 2 Journaling for Success

Once you take the time to sit down and write out what you want out of this journey, you'll begin to realize how compelling the process of writing is to your success. You can go back and read your thoughts (make sure to date each entry) so that you can measure and adjust for your progress.

And now that you've started with the Goal Setting (you started, right?) here's the next thing you're going to want to do…

Write down EVERYTHING that goes into your mouth for the next 7 days. Everything. Food, drink, dessert…everything.

We both know that nutrition is going to be a key factor in your successful training. The problem most of us have is that we THINK we eat properly. Putting a diary together…for just a week…is going to be very telling, and sometimes a little shocking.

That little diary is going to give you an actual look at your lifestyle and a nudge if changes are necessary. Hint: They probably will be. Just sayin'.

Back to the diary: giving yourself a good look at 'a week in the life' is a great way to help create the plan that is most beneficial to your fitness goals.

Do it.

4

Chapter 3 Lifestyle: What is Yours?

Back to Lou for a minute.

As you might imagine, someone working a trading desk has a pretty stressful job, as would his co-workers. Lou and his buddies didn't skip too many happy hours or appetizers during the after-work part of the day, hence the 'Dunlap'. Weekends weren't much better, oftentimes socializing with like-minded neighbors and friends.

Football season was especially challenging, although at the time, 'challenging' probably wasn't what was going through Lou's mind. Lou's wife (Tammy) was right there with him, and eventually, she also paid the price of indulgence. We'll get to her later.

Not quite a rabbit trail, but it was the invention of the cell phone that caused Lou to decide to change his lifestyle. You can probably guess why. Those pictures from years ago...sans the double chins and spare tire. Yup; that did it.

Point being: it's easy to get caught up in this kind of merry-go-round, but a lot of people never get off. That's not you, right? That's why you're still reading because you've decided to take control of your life and make a few changes. Right?

Good answer.

You don't need to go all monk to achieve your fitness goals. You can still have your cheat days, just not as often, maybe once a week or so. There's a great book on a lifestyle that lets you have the cheat days while being your best self, fitness-wise, called "Burn the Fat, Feed the Muscle" by Tom Veneto. Highly recommended.

Just understand that no matter how hard you workout in the gym, an over-indulgent lifestyle will negate all that effort. No need to knowingly self-destruct your journey.

To paraphrase Nancy Reagan: just say 'no'. Most of the time, that is.

Chapter 4 You Need These

I f you don't already have one (and it's shocking if you don't), get a good scale. Not a cheapo, a good one. This is you we're talking about and you're worth it.

Plan on stepping on it once a week, the same day at about the same time. I find my best time is first thing in the morning before I eat or drink anything.

And, yes, write it down.

You probably don't have one of these, but you'll need it. Fat calipers. Fat testers. Different names for the same thing: a little do-hickey that will measure your percentage of body fat. "Accu-Measure" is one brand that will provide you with the tool and a guide to figure out just how well you're progressing on your fitness journey.

Right after you get off the scale, grab the calipers and measure. You'll take a fold of skin just above your hip, put the squeeze on the caliper, and get the number. Do it three or four times to make sure you get a consistent result and then consult the guide. It's segmented by gender and age into groups. Find your group to determine your percentage of body fat.

This is where your math skills come into play. Divide your body weight by the percentage and voila: this is approximately how much body fat vs. lean muscle you have.

And, yes, write it down. Each week. You can make a spreadsheet and fill it out each week to see your progress and keep you motivated to stay on track.

Lou was kind enough to let us use a copy of his first 2 months' progress; it's at the end of the book.

Seriously: these are really great tools for your journey. But you know that. Just get them.

Chapter 5 Nutrition

A worthy topic that deserves a bit more attention. A good portion of the people who get this book are looking to lose weight along with gaining strength; hence the need to touch upon nutrition.

That said, this isn't going to be a detailed guide on nutrition; there are plenty of them out there.

But just as a quick observation, we are beginning to see a rather substantial shift in thinking in terms of how and why we get fat. And it's no longer calories in vs. calories out as we've been told for decades. It seems that the main culprit is carbohydrates. Shocker, I know.

Everyone is aware of the problem with carbohydrates; there are good ones and bad ones. Apparently, the bad ones are foods most refined, and not so coincidentally, the ones we most crave: pasta, pastries, sweets... you know this dance. We all do.

The easy answer is to avoid those horrible, delicious things. Easier said than done. However, if you really want to delve into this subject more deeply, I recommend reading the book "Why We Get Fat" by Gary Taubes. An interesting read, written so that the layman won't get lost in the weeds of technical jargon. If you do take the time, you may find a new level of motivation to help avoid those horrible, delicious carbs.

While we're touching on nutrition, be advised that numerous experts are big proponents of the carnivore diet and swear by its effectiveness in terms of weight loss and muscle gain. Just keep that in mind as you go about building strength.

Chapter 6 Water, Vitamins, Minerals and Supplements

A gain, no surprises here: water is your magic elixir. Drink it, and drink it often. Have at least a 16-ounce bottle with you when you hit the gym and don't be shy about having more. Depending on the authority, we're told to drink...I don't know, a lot of water each day. But it's good advice, and we'll file that under 'Duh'.

However, the conversation about vitamins, minerals, and supplements can go on and on, seemingly ad infinitum. A good multivitamin will take care of most all essential needs and there are many available specifically for men and women. Additional doses of Vitamin D and B12 are also a good idea. Given the paucity of vitamins in many of the manufactured foods that we still eat, it's practically a no-brainer to bring our own into the mix.

As far as minerals and supplements are concerned: get some magnesium, it's a godsend for muscle cramps. Nitric oxide, glucosamine, and potassium are also good teammates to have on your side. Protein shakes are trickier; some experts have become a little skeptical about whey proteins, while others are still firmly supporting whey. Your choice. Check to see what kind of sweeteners are being used; stevia or monk fruit are OK. Almost every manufacturer of protein powder also offers 'pre-workout' formulas, something typically mixed with water or other beverages and consumed 15-30 minutes prior to hitting the weights. Be careful with these, as they are stimulants and can really get your engine revving.

Back to Lou and his experience.

Prior to beginning his journey, Lou had his primary physician do a complete blood work-up. He learned a few things about his metabolism that actually helped him make some necessary changes to both his strength training plan and more importantly, his lifestyle. Turned out that he was pre-diabetic and was able to make changes in time to put a stop to that trip. If you've got a good primary care physician you should have no trouble requesting similar testing and it's recommended that you do so.

8

Chapter 7 Injuries: Avoid Them! Also Filed Under 'Duh'

O nce again, this is easier said than done, especially if you haven't been in the gym for a while. Just starting up again is pretty much a guarantee that you'll at least be sore where you haven't been sore for a long time. Welcome the sore; it means that something good is happening. And if it's just sore, it goes away pretty quickly...assuming that you keep at it. There's no quit in you, so that's not a consideration. Right?

The trick is to recognize the difference between muscle soreness and injury. You may be thinking that an injury is obviously different, but that's not always the case. Elbow pain, for example, might fool you into thinking that it's just soreness when it could be more serious, such as bursitis. Be careful.

The best strategy is to approach weight training using your head, not your ego.

Remember that journal you started? You're going to write down your workout before you begin. You'll write down how many reps you want to get per set and how much rest you'll take between sets. You'll write down the body part that will get attention and which exercise you'll use. You'll determine how much weight you start with, and how much weight on subsequent sets. At the end, you'll decide on your RPE (rate of perceived exertion) using a scale of 1-10, with 10 being the hardest.

An example:

(*Goal*):8-10 reps 90 seconds rest (between sets) RPE: (*upon completion of sets*) 10
   Chest: Bench Press

   1. 100#- 10 reps 2. 100-10 3. 110-7

You'll do this for each movement on each body part and refer to it the next time you're doing that particular exercise.

RPE= rate of perceived exertion is your estimate of how hard you had to work to complete the sets. A rating of 10 means that you couldn't get all the desired reps out. Not a bad thing; it means that you're doing the work. A rating of less than 8 means you're slacking. Add some weight.

Here's where you AVOID injury: Use your head, not your ego. In this case, if you can cleanly complete the repetition—not half a rep, not a quarter rep—a complete rep, and you can do it for your own pre-determined goals, then you can move up. And because you used proper form—the clean rep—you can be reasonably confident of avoiding injury.

Almost every injury I've ever seen in the gym comes from "exuberance".

That's my diplomatic way of saying "stupidity".

Control your exuberance.

Now, that doesn't mean you shouldn't be feeling it after; soreness can be a good indicator that your muscles are growing. A little trick from some veteran gym rats: use a little pain relief cream or liquid before you hit the gym. Aspercream and Voltarin are a couple of brand names that are quite effective, and there are plenty of off-brands that work as well. Shoulders, elbows, knees, and lower back seem to be the most frequent areas that will thank you for the pre-emptive treatment.

Chapter 8 The Workouts: Let's Get Down to It!

G ive yourself a few minutes to stretch out and warm up your muscles. The clock doesn't start ticking on your workout until after the warm-up.

Beginning Plan: 3 Days per Week

This is for the person just returning to the routine. Build up to a 4 or even 6-day-per-week schedule once your body becomes acclimated to your new journey.

Whether you're doing 3, 4, or even 6 days a week workouts, always try to keep the workouts close to 45 minutes, not including your warmup. Research has shown that exertion past 45 minutes in our age group provides declining benefit, to the point that it's more beneficial to keep a time limit.

Rabbit Trail (not really, just kind of):

This has to do with a little something called 'gym etiquette', a topic that should be addressed by every gym in the world when a person signs up. In essence, unless you are there at 3 a.m. and all alone...there are other people working out. Be considerate. If you need to use the dumbbells, take them off the rack and step away so that others can access the rack. If you are using free weights, strip the bar and return the plates to the rack when you're finished. Wipe the equipment down when you're through. If you're at a particular station, do the sets and move along; no lollygagging when other people are waiting for the equipment. If someone is using a mirror to monitor their form–don't get in the way! Mostly, what we're talking about here is the Golden Rule. Treat others as you would have them treat you. Very big point in the gym.

OK, back to our regularly scheduled program:

Beginning Plan: 3 Days per Week

Monday (3) sets each	Wednesday (3) sets each	Friday (*) sets
Chest	Thighs	Chest (3)
Back	Deltoids	Back (3)
Bicep	Tricep	Thighs (3)
Calf	Abs	Calf (2)
		Deltoid (2)
		Tricep (2)
		Bicep (2)
12-15 reps	12-15 reps	8-10 reps
2 minutes rest	2 minutes rest	2 minute rest

(This is where Tammy came into the picture. Seeing Lou's enthusiasm and determination to turn back the clock got her caught up. She did her pre-planning for her journey and joined Lou in the gym. And Lou learned a little something else about training: working with a partner made it that much easier to keep to a schedule. Win-win.)

Some suggested exercises for these days:

Chest: Bench Press, Inclined Bench Press, Decline Bench Press, Dumbbell Fly Flat, Dumbbell Fly Incline, Dumbbell Fly Decline, Inverted Row, Decline Pushup

Back: Low Cable Row, Wide Grip Cable Pull-down, Narrow Grip Cable Pull-down, Dumbbell Lawnmowers, Cable Flys Straight, Cable Flys Bent Over, Deadlift, Bent Over Row

Bicep: EZ Curl Wide Grip, EZ Curl Narrow Grip, Dumbbell Hammer Curl/Straight/Articulated/Crossover, Assisted Pullups/Unassisted Pullup/Various Grips, Cable Curls/Wide/Narrow Grip, Preacher Curl w/EZ Curl Bar

Calf: Calf Press, Calf Extension, Weighted Calf Raises

Thighs: Barbell Squats, Bulgarian Split Squats, Leg Extensions

Deltoids: Dumbbell Lateral Raise, Dumbbell Bent-over Lateral Raise, Dumbbell Front Raise, Dumbbell Lawnmowers, Straight Seat Pull-downs

Tricep: Close Grip Bench Press, EZ Curl Close Grip Bench Press, Cable Tri-downs, Dumbbell Kick-backs, Assisted Dips/Unassisted Dips/Wide and Narrow Grip

Abs: Mountain Climbers, Knee-ups, Ball Twists, Hanging Knee-ups

Note: "_Some_ suggested exercises" means just that; there are plenty more available that you probably already know. We'll put a couple of diagrams in later of the ones that may be unfamiliar because of the name. Once you see them you'll say to yourself: "oh, that's what that's called."

You may be curious as to why you've been given a choice (your choice, not mine) as to which exercise you'll do for individual body parts. Good question.

Part of the secret to success on this journey is to avoid plateaus in your workouts, something that happens when the body gets used to the same movements used repeatedly. The solution is to confuse the body by mixing up the movements on a regular basis. The recommendation is to alternate movements around 4-6 weeks after starting them.

In other words, you may decide that your chest workout will be the bench press, a fine choice. However, after about 4 weeks or so of benching, try something different. Use a dumbbell workout, or switch to an incline position. Continue with switching movements and you'll continue to see improvement.

As a reminder, it is important to your success that you document EVERYTHING that you do during these workouts; sets, reps, rate of exertion (RPE). This will not just chart your progress, it will bring you in line with Albert Einstein.

Albert Einstein? "How" you ask. Simple. Albert claimed that he never memorized anything that he could look up.

It's the same with your journal. This will tell you how you're doing, and serve as your reminder to switch up your protocols.

If this is where you started, do this plan for 3 or 4 weeks to get your body acclimated to the routine and then make the call.

Feeling pretty good? Ready to move up? OK, here's a 4 days per week plan:

Monday	Tuesday	Thursday	Friday
(4) sets	(4) sets	(*) sets	(*) sets
Back	Thighs	Back (4)	Thighs (4)
Chest	Deltoid	Chest (4)	Chest (4)
Bicep	Tricep	Thighs (4)	Back (4)
Calf	Abs	Deltoid(2)	Deltoid (2)
		Calf (2)	Calf (2)
		Bicep (1)	Tricep (1)
		Tricep (1)	Bicep (1)
12-15 reps	12-15 reps	8-10 reps	6-8 reps
90 seconds rest each day			

Note that the beginning of the week is geared toward endurance and requires more repetitions per set. Obviously, and you know this, more repetitions means using less weight. As you get on into the week, the reps will drop and this is where you'll increase the weight. That's the power phase for all you Hulksters and Wonder Women.

In the 6-day plan, those two more days are going to become a tipping point in your strength training journey...and you know what that means. Grrr...

Remember! Form is everything, and that includes a complete rep! Don't let them call you "half-a-rep", as *that is not a compliment*. If you can't do a complete rep, decrease the weight! Remember: use your head, not your ego.

You should have noticed that some body part workouts are repeated without a day's rest, something that has been frowned upon since forever. The funny thing is (well, not funny; informative) that Bulgarian trainers (mad weightlifters and highly respected worldwide) determined that a muscle can be trained 5 hours after it has been stressed. They also determined that a muscle group will begin to atrophy after 72 hours of no stress. (Not to worry, citations will follow.) Therefore, it's perfectly OK to repeat a muscle group the next day. And once you get into a routine, don't let more than 3 days go by without some activity!

Let's look at a 6-day workout plan.

6 Days per Week

	Monday	Tuesday	Wednesday	Thursday	Friday	Saturday
4 Sets	Back	Deltoid	Chest	Deltoid	Back	Deltoid
	Chest	Tricep	Back	Tricep	Chest	Tricep
	Bicep	Thighs	Biceps	Thighs	Calf	Thighs
	Calf	Abs	Calf	Abs	Bicep	Abs
90 Seconds Rest						
Repetitions	13 to 15	13 to 15	10 to 12	10 to 12	8 to 10	8 to 10

All the plans shown are designed to give you options beyond just the individual exercises.

As you progress and improve, don't be reluctant to add sets to the daily routines or mix up the rest periods. Once you really get into a groove, challenge yourself by adding repetitions to the endurance days.

Go from 12-15 to 25-30 for the larger muscle groups, and even more reps for the smaller groups, such as biceps and triceps. Decrease the repetitions on the power days and increase the weight. Go for the 'pump'; might as well see the improvement since you'll be working so hard.

Chapter 9 Motivation

Motivation comes from within, no matter what people tell you. Sure, we have people like Tony Robbins that will get you jazzed up, but really, that's because you want to get jazzed up. Strength training is something very personal, and you've got to decide that you want it. That's why the initial planning is so critical. Knowing the 'why' of any endeavor you choose to do is the difference between simply going through the motions or taking home the grand prize. Take home the grand prize. You deserve it.

Now that you're in it, there are a few tricks that you already have in your bag to keep you focused:

The journal. This is a valuable tool that you'll refer to daily to record what you did in the gym that day. Next week when it's time to do leg extensions again, you'll look back and see what you did the last time. You're going to want to at least match that and more than likely improve upon it. You are competing against yourself and you have to win. Can you imagine teasing yourself for losing? Makes no sense, so get that last rep. But seriously, using your journal as a reference point is a great way to keep yourself on track and keep on keeping on.

The scale *and* fat loss spreadsheet (there's Lou's example at the end of the book). Lou's record was slow and steady, as you'll see from the sheet. One of the big benefits of recording your weight from week to week is the implicit nutritional guidance. You'll be more aware of what's going in the pie-hole each day and act accordingly. As far as Lou was concerned: After a year, he was teasing with 200 as a body weight and got there after his 13th month. He's still sticking with the program and is firmly in the 190s today with a very healthy 17% body fat (and missing 'Dunlap'). Tammy didn't want to share her progress (women, go figure) but she's done a great job and looks fabulous. A great looking couple, for sure. And still doing their training dates...leading to the next:

Have or get a training partner. Having a training partner is one of the best motivational tools at your disposal. Knowing that someone else is counting on you to simply be there is surprisingly effective at getting you there. Soon enough, an obligation becomes an opportunity and something to look forward to. Strength training is hard work, let's not kid ourselves, and it can be tempting to rationalize a skip day. But this kind of hard work pays great dividends and can be a lot of fun. Lou was doing OK at the beginning of his journey, but once Tammy got involved it became a visible acceleration for both of them. Their workouts became a date that they both really enjoyed. If you can get on a schedule with a training partner, by all means, do so.

The mirror. Need we say more? OK, we'll say more. The mirror is more than likely the reason you chose to begin this journey in the first place. We want to like what we see when staring at the looking glass, and as you progress and improve...you will appreciate the improvement. Go ahead and flex those biceps, they look great. But you should probably know that the real working power is in the triceps, so flex those, too. And if you have two mirrors working, then you'll get a good idea of how you look from behind. Use the mirror; it's your friend on this journey.

<u>Your 'why'</u>. Perhaps the key motivator in the entire bag of tricks. You need to know 'why' you chose to take this journey, and that's something only you understand. And that's the reason you have been strongly encouraged to think about it and WRITE IT DOWN. There are going to be days when you just don't have that oomph to get your backside down to the gym, and those are the days you need to review your thinking. There's a country song whose lyrics repeat "What was I thinking?" as they describe some questionable choices. In this case, reviewing "What was I thinking?" is going to be the switch that keeps you focused on the new and improved you.

Don't worry; you got this.

11

Notes, Illustrations and Citations

H ere's Lou's chart of progress for body fat reduction for the first two months of his journey. Slow and steady makes for the best long-term improvements that stay with you.

Date	Body Weight	Skinfold (mm)	Bodyfat %	Fat Weight	Lean Weight
5/2/2022	247.6	18	26	64.38	183.22
5/9/2022	245.5	18	26	63.83	181.67
5/16/2022	243.2	17	24.5	59.58	183.6
5/23/2022	240.7	17	24.5	58.97	181.7
5/30/2022	238.1	16	24.5	58.33	179.8
6/6/2022	235.9	15	22.8	53.8	182.1
6/13/2022	232	14	22.8	52.9	179.1
6/20/2022	228.4	13	21	48	180.4
6/27/2022	226.9	13	21	47.6	179.25

And here are a few illustrations of exercises that you may not be familiar with.

Bulgarian Split Squat

Inverted Row

Incline Dumbbell Fly

Dumbbell Bent-over Lateral Raise

12

Conclusion

I hope that you have found this book to be useful and entertaining.

I intentionally did not get into the weeds about any topic. My intent in writing this was to provide a bird's-eye view of strength training and the importance of incorporating a mental aspect into any program.

If you enjoyed this, please leave me a positive review.

If you didn't...please don't. I need good reviews.

PJ Rae 9/2023

Pictured below: The Author and his Grandchild

13

References and Credits

1. *Burn the Fat, Feed the Muscle* by Tom Veneto: guidance on body fat measurement and exercise illustrations
2. Silverback Muscle Building Guide by Leo Costa and Dr. Russ Horine: information on Bulgarian training studies as well as initial workout guidance
3. *Why We Get Fat* by Gary Taubes: information on nutrition studies, carbohydrates, and carnivore diet

Made in the USA
Las Vegas, NV
15 December 2023

82886756R00024